LIVE ONES

OSKANA POETRY & POETICS

Sadie McCarney

*Live Ones*

University of Regina Press

© 2019 Sadie McCarney

All rights reserved. No part of this work covered by the copyrights hereon may be reproduced or used in any form or by any means—graphic, electronic, or mechanical—without the prior written permission of the publisher. Any request for photocopying, recording, taping or placement in information storage and retrieval systems of any sort shall be directed in writing to Access Copyright.

Cover art: *Winged Skull / Memento Mori* by Susan Crawford.

Cover and text design: Duncan Campbell, University of Regina Press

Editor: Laurie D. Graham
Proofreader: Donna Grant

The text and titling faces are Arno, designed by Robert Slimbach.

*Library and Archives Canada Cataloguing in Publication*

Title: Live ones / Sadie McCarney.

Names: McCarney, Sadie, 1992- author.

Series: Oskana poetry & poetics.

Description: Series statement: Oskana poetry & poetics | Poems.

Identifiers: Canadiana (print) 20190113448 | Canadiana (ebook) 20190113464 | ISBN 9780889776500 (softcover) | ISBN 9780889776753 (hardcover) | ISBN 9780889776517 (PDF) | ISBN 9780889776524 (HTML)

Classification: LCC PS8625.C37436 L58 2019 | DDC C811/.6—dc23

UNIVERSITY OF REGINA PRESS
University of Regina
Regina, Saskatchewan
Canada S4S 0A2
TELEPHONE: (306) 585-4758
FAX: (306) 585-4699
WEB: www.uofrpress.ca
EMAIL: uofrpress@uregina.ca

We acknowledge the support of the Canada Council for the Arts for our publishing program. We acknowledge the financial support of the Government of Canada. / Nous reconnaissons l'appui financier du gouvernement du Canada. This publication was made possible with support from Creative Saskatchewan's Book Publishing Production Grant Program.

*In memory of Art & Dot MacPherson, my early dead*

## CONTENTS

- 1  Answer and Be Entered to Win
- 2  Early Adopters
- 5  First Death in Nova Scotia, 1997
- 6  Bee Funeral
- 7  Last Summer at Melmerby Beach
- 9  The Incredibles
- 11  Steeltown Songs
- 19  Revival
- 20  Step—
- 22  13
- 23  Home Bus
- 24  Unscattered
- 26  The Battle Re-enactors' Edda
- 28  $90K Victorian, Sold As Is
- 29  Blue-heads
- 30  The Toucan
- 32  The Surgical Theatre
- 33  Night Lunch
- 35  Man to Man
- 37  Elegy for Baby Girl
- 39  Milford
- 41  Blight
- 43  Biology Major Field Notes, 1974
- 45  Wedding, Late Summer
- 47  Fairy Tale in the Supermarket
- 49  Moon, Moon, Earth
- 52  Hoarders: Valley of the Kings
- 54  Analytics
- 55  Nurse Ouch
- 57  House, Kept
- 58  Receiving
- 60  Spring Catalogue
- 62  The Dead of Winter

## ANSWER AND BE ENTERED TO WIN

*a found poem culled from dating site questionnaires*

In a potential mate, do 14 marriages
matter? Do you like your pit hair?

Are you a virgin? Do you ever
masturbate to spelling mistakes?

Are food stamps a turn-on? Are
*you* a turn-on? Would you wear

a dildo as everyday clothes?
How do you feel about policemen

with illegal whips and chains?
Should murderers shave? Should

voluptuous women be allowed to
park in handicapped spaces? Could

prostitutes take advantage of war?
Has anyone ever accused you

of talking? Are you jealous of men
in horror movies? Ever *been* jealous?

Ever been Jewish? Do you believe we
share a common ancestor with God?

In the right light, wouldn't primates be
sexy? In the right light, wouldn't anyone be?

## EARLY ADOPTERS

Both your moms were in line, #243
and #244, the day of the Black
Friday sale "so good you couldn't

conceive of it!" as the preying
clickbait ads proclaimed. The lineup
was dotted with camp chairs (Evenflo

bottles expectant in their armrest
mesh) and Coleman coolers full
of lab-made breast milk (like the slurry

your moms found online from
the States). In the whole line, hope:
the first 300 had each been

promised a kid, including
the polygamous cult beyond
town and the old, the poor,

the rejects from local adoption
rounds. #243 and #244 had lived
the horror along with the rest

when the once-fertile town's life-sap
dried up and took the yearly
births along with it. A desperate

decade since, the former doulas now
data admins, the round jungle gyms
like spit-out Gobstoppers. Your moms

had all the arguments twice. They
figured out who would be "Mommy,"
who "Mumma," set a schedule

around #244's work. No to dolls but
yes to attachment parenting, parks,
puréed green peas. #243 wore

a papoose full of black beans
to mimic your bulk like she birthed
you herself. They loved you long

before Black Friday.

                      The overnight
stock clerk stared them all down
and the mass of 300 all hushed

like a church, steeling themselves
for the great sprint inside. "They're
all asleep!" he bellowed, grey-faced,

"so you'll have to be quiet!" A tiptoe
doorcrasher. #243 and #244, your moms,
exchanged a look, because What if—

but then the bullhorn! And they lost
each other in the furious stampede.
Everywhere legs and flailing arms,

and #243 ran like they'd rehearsed,
dodging limbs all different colours—
each unique shade of desperation.

She found you in a bassinet, sable-
hued and somehow sleeping amid
the surrounding Armageddon,

so she tucked you tight against
her, swaddled in your celestial-print
blankie, and ran. There was no hope

of making it to the cash without the mob
taking you, tearing apart the you-bundle
now quivering against her. So she ran

and mercifully made it to the un-
manned front doors, the fresh air…
#243 rubbernecked around now,

panicked. There were the cultists
(thieves like her) but where *was* she,
your Mumma? Where was her love?

Where was #244?

## FIRST DEATH IN NOVA SCOTIA, 1997

Nick (the *not right* neighbour boy)
says, "Shootin' fliers," so I'm coming.
In eye-high grass he shows off his toy
pellet gun and tackle box of dried wings
as butterflies puff from the yard like dust.
"Cabbage whites," Nick grins. "Real common."
They flit like shapes I forgot I'd traced
in air, until his zigzag aim hits one.
It wrecks the 'fros of dandelions.
Squint-eyed and with Gran's good tweezers,
Nick plucks butterfly bits from the lawn
to sort them into clear containers
neat and safe as correctional cells.
*Not right.* Crisp antennae, scales.

## BEE FUNERAL

In fifth grade Crybaby and Almost-
Boobs hoarded curios in a Kleenex
box: hunks of rock shaped like
pizza slices, gel pens' worn-out

tips. Crud. That summer behind
the dugout they found the body:
like seppuku, the bumblebee had
stung itself dead. So Crybaby

and Almost-Boobs became funeral
directors. From their Kleenex box
they got a monogrammed hankie
for its shroud, its coffin a torn-up

tarot box from Almost-Boobs' Wiccan
babysitter. Crybaby held in her aquifer
of tears even though it almost geysered
(like when she forgot her lunch, or

fell down). But what would a bee need
to pack like a sack lunch, for whatever
might be coming after? Crybaby gave
it flowers: a broken dollar-store lei,

daisy stickers, a stemless silk rose.
For a marker, Crybaby and Almost-
Boobs suckled pink Popsicles, made
a cross with the sticks. That fall

Almost-Boobs became Boobs. She
began to date Boyfriend 1, quit their
Kleenex box full of tinsel and crud.
Crybaby cried. The bumblebees flew.

## LAST SUMMER AT MELMERBY BEACH

Like troops we round the bluff,
half the family, goose-step over

poison oak and rickety stairs.
We lug chairs, the ostentatious

umbrella big as a flowered igloo.
Someone's new iPod bleats out

"Everything's Alright" from *Jesus
Christ Superstar*. An uncle's Nikon

winks as seagulls scavenge half
a sandwich from its crust of sand.

The last Great Aunt is the last
to disembark from the Lincoln

Town Car with her rock-a-bye gait,
skin thin and marbled as vellum.

By now her innards are carved up
by the cancer, metastasized every

way like the night's last firework.
Ablaze, and then dead. She knows

she's come on the Farewell Tour,
to dip the tip of her violet-tinged

foot in the Atlantic and breathe deep
its saltwater spray for the first time,

the last time. Her kids rub Coppertone
snake oil on to broil with their towels,

the marram teased out like a big
hairdo on the dunes. Her kids' kids take

driftwood spears and hoist jellyfish
to taunt just-met cousins. (Every-

thing's alright, yes, everything's fine!)
We all clap as the Nikon captures

her step into seawater, the sandbar
crunchy with dulse. Her toe taps

the frigid surf that laps at the shore
like she might dance away from us.

Somewhere far. Somewhere else.

THE INCREDIBLES

I wear this worn-out
comforter like a cape.
On my greasy 12-year-
old head: a kitchen
colander, 6 pillows
gone flat as old pop.

In this game it's a helmet.
In this game I see a bullet
streak past while the ex-
superhero dad on TV
gradually takes up his old
post again because he

misses the adrenaline
thrill, the risk. In this
game the bullet misses
me by an inch. Because
I'm wearing my protective
helmet I don't see the end

of our Blockbuster rental,
when the whole family
teams up to save the world.
In this game Dad tells me
like a weird Hail Mary that
it wasn't a bullet, just a rock,

*just a rock*! In this game
we find the rock and watch
the credits, watch each
other. Watch the trembling,
bad-neighbourhood dad
who thought for a minute

this thing with the gun
and his kid was all real.

## STEELTOWN SONGS

I.

All down the conveyor, the limes
bumped ends with a banged-up
mango and my checkout nerves.
Off work, soon. And then another

BOGO week, my lip gloss layered
on like sealant, a week of soap and fat
onion sacks hefted high to haggle
their worth. Nothing else to watch

but gas blots in a grimy overhang
of light, where a caravan of cabs
wear lit-up caps and idle more
smoke at smokers' backs.

II.

Sometimes the Axe®-doused
after-school stock boys tackle
shelves with the force of a tag team,
sweaty and boastful in their show-off skill.

Brings it all back, though whether
it's them or just piss-warm coolant
from the on/off AC, I couldn't say.
It's like ghost pains in a gangrened limb:

to spar with them! to flex with pumped-up steroid
pecs and vault them into the vertigo of ceiling tiles!
(All sense slashed by *4061 lettuce, 4041 plums,*
 and an old recognition that dawns on me like drink.)

III.

The new bruised limes bump on past
checkout, and I stutter "cash-debit-credit,"
then see: spit-thin girl. A spastic 16,
nearer to bald and pitted by pockmarks,

who still watches worms ooze fatly in rain,
still skips a hopscotch to the chimes
on poor porches. Prue. Same grin—toothy,
lean of love—still half-stirring some

cops-and-robbers cool, half-known through
the soft swells of a roughed-up decade.
She is gaunt as spare rib in the
disaffected drought of June. Older, now.

IV.

Back then, me and Prue were coyotes.
Spooked mean and scrapping into fights,
we spat like it was our sole tiff with the mud-
plugged stone. Played tag, too, with the boys

(in roles, always Bad Guys or Mounties),
imagined other selves we'd rather be
jailed in for a quarter-hour twice daily. Back
in that cramped neighbourhood of knives,

Four Square was the thing each weekday:
a mangy tennis ball matted by dog drool
and hit over chalked-in lines. And dirt above all,
ingrained in denim, dusting a tanned crust of skin.

v.

Thursday Night Smackdown. These were
pay-per-view poets, gods of powdered cheese
and TV takedowns, and I knew war was a need
of skin. Broken bodies got tried on daily

like shin pads, mouth guards, never quite fitting
no matter how much their shapes got stretched
to *make* them fit. There were lives beyond lives,
sands beyond my little slit of beach and beer glass.

Wanted to earn belts myself someday. Or box,
The Meanest Bantamweight East of Toronto,
my triceps emboldened by barbells, blood,
and a bluish cancer courtesy of Maritime Steel.

VI.

Sometimes we skipped our chalked-in court,
our tire swing's welts of spit-out gum. Mondays
the dawn mist of strangers' pot did it—too much
bitter in the smell of sweet. Or too much sweet.

On those days we followed the ripped-up main road
like alley cats, strays mewing loudly for bones.
Past the dark, bloated bellies of trash bags brimming
with meat scraps, past chipped paint and chokeweed,

we wandered where train tracks scarred the town.
I dug for rail spikes loosed by boxcars while Prue
eyed the dank front of the building behind: self-storage
doors like little garages rusted shut and let lie for years.

VII.

Mildew, damp earth, plywood for windows,
a thin fire escape of warped grey boards.
Gang tags advertised the safety of standing,
so we left the earth and its spray-on bruises behind

to climb until ears popped and we saw in panorama.
The whole town: musty churches, the Liquor Commission,
and blue banks where the river swam its current
to trees. No rail, so we helped each other higher,

rocked like planes redirecting in air *higher*,
past gutters and patched-up doors. Busted boards
swayed below us like seesaws. Facing left: our North End,
the used mattress shop with just a bare spring on display.

VIII.

We saw it all: home, on Clover and Worth,
where the prefabs were mostly built of Insulbrick
and gin. Crushed-up cans in the mealy oaks.
There, we were one stock, whiteblackredbroke.

When the dizzy bloodrush of too much height
got Prue and we started to crawl back groundward,
we both thought past town lines we couldn't see.
And what might grow there. Dragged legs to Kwik-Way

where found change paid for half the counter:
nickel each for neon straws and grape-shaped gobs
dipped in sour sugar. Squinted hard and puckered
as we sucked. Like steeling for punches. Or for a kiss.

REVIVAL

It was like a diorama of end-times
life, that grizzled strip of no man's

land between our apartment and
the Masonic Lodge. Always with

a capsized shopping cart, ripped
grocery bags that billowed in the wind.

Always that stubborn hunk of snow
and silt in mid-July. And over it all,

the shimmer of smashed beer bottles
like low-rent stardust, community glitter.

The Masons must have done some rite;
overnight we found the spot transformed

with tent pegs and ropes, a rented sound
system and a nylon marquee so white

it could have caused snow blindness.
The neo-Baptists' subwoofers warbled

out hymns and prayers all morning. But they
got garbled for us: *Jesus hugs bees*, a few

hallelujahs. *You've gotta let go, and let go.*

STEP—

We were all there: crows,
prim diaconal priest,
third cousins wound tight
together like cornrows.

Two by two, like school-
kids, we filed past the deceased
tarted up in her box,
a bad kewpie doll

with too much rouge.
She never looked so alive
in life, like she'd cancan dance
if you gave her a nudge.

The second wives and I hived
together like bees, abuzz
with idle laughs and chatter—
politics, who brought which bread.

We were all step-aunts
or step-something-or-others,
ghosts the family kept
like cats to haunt

and haunt the family tree.
In a six-foot furrow
they hoisted her down
(cold dirt dry as liturgy)

in silk and blue eyeshadow
(although, alive, she'd shunned
running water). They recalled
her hugs, a stale waft of tobacco.

But we married in. We weren't
the Hummel figurines or pudgy
granddaughter she loved. We ate
date squares and stared at our feet.

The dead, but once or twice removed.

# 13

and this airplane's the size of an aphid who'll prey on the fresh condos of suburban Boston; 13 and I'm wearing my too-big jeans, stinky and inked over in ballpoint pen; 13 and my suitcase is packed with Nair and tarot I pretend I can use; 13 and I predict her hair will already be greying and unwashed yet perfect; 13 and she'll smoke the stubs of clove cigarettes snug in black wrappers like jackets; 13 and I'll tell the whole room I drink as I take my very first swig of liquor; 13 and I'll ache to be dared to kiss her; 13 and she'll say she's been to alternate states on LSD, on coke, on speed; 13 and there will never be an alternate Massachusetts where I do not love her; 13 and I won't know much about hormones, but I'll understand kabooms and chemical reactions; 13 and I'll nurse a chemical burn from the Nair I only slather on to impress her; 13 and the outdoor summer stock theatre will be so hot someone faints in front of us; 13 and she'll be that hot, too, but right now this airplane's so small my limbs are tucked in for rescue, and with my square inch of space I pull a Bic from my pocket and colour a blue-black heart on my jeans (keeping the warm pen snug in my hand) because I don't know any of this yet; I'm 13 and flying for the very first time and I don't know what it feels like to land.

HOME BUS

*Why should she believe the road*
*she came on was not always road…?*

    —RICHARD HUGO, "Schoolgirl at Seola"

A Pictou June differs little: '80s hair bands
and a halitosis breeze from the mill.
If you pointed out the pell-mell redwoods
or Chev mausoleums covered in moss,
she'd hardly hear. Like conchs,
her headphones sound a new sea.

Past "2 miles!" signs for ghost pit stops
and numerous lupins' purple pricks,
the farms grow thin. The scrapyard,
the deer, and finally Axl Rose shows her
the house: greasy windows, the blind
black cat, the bus's low grind of grace.

## UNSCATTERED

He told us: throw his ashes "backabents,"
and we nodded, just as if we'd understood.
But then the cancer spread, as every synapse went,
and along with them, our way to find that wood.

Did he mean "back of Bent's"? Was this Bent
a man on whose land he'd trespassed,
like Peter Rabbit past McGregor's fence?
Could zigzag genealogy help us find the rest?

Or was "backabents" a nickname the colliers' sons
all gave to some secret glade they shared,
free from the coal dust that coated their lungs,
with wars and blood pacts enacted there?

"Backabents." Are we sure he didn't make it up?
He tricked his shrivelled tulips back to bloom,
held baby dolls *and* car brochures on his lap,
whistled sweet solos, and yelled. His makeshift tomb

brims with contradiction—how could a puny box
of wood hold him, a man capricious as a goat?
For he raged, sang, ironed pleats in his slacks,
and made succulent stew dumplings. Now he is grit

and ash—no more Tim's coffee twice a day,
no more buoyant bass solos in choirs' anthems.
There's nothing left of him to feel dismay
we never found the place of his enchantment,

"backabents." *He* might have known those woods.
We couldn't mark the spot, grew gaunt with guilt.
But even had we found the place and done it, could
we really bring the old man peace by pitching silt?

## THE BATTLE RE-ENACTORS' EDDA

They called a truce to the artificial war
too late. By the time the black-powder

boss dislodged his neon earplugs &
the last British shot felled a local

custodian who cussed & spurted
convincing red, both hobbyist

regiments were overrun. Never mind
the French soldier with the Indiglo

watch who'd lost half his hand in a meat
grinder's maw, & whose this-weekend

wife unwrapped ice packs from her tits
as she simmered a pot of fake blood

for the troops. Never mind iPhones,
plastic baggies of lunch. The gore

from the ornamental guns was enough.
Like zaps of lightning the zaftig woman-

beasts came, grey-winged, their white-
blonde hair like heads full of swords.

Their breastplates shone bronze in
the noon-hour sun. The encampment

cowered while these eerie shieldmaidens
dredged up the "dead" in their muscular

arms, the faux-French-and-English,
winging them back to Valhalla, barrel-

aged mead, & bed. The "dead" howled
so, the Valkyries heard them even above

the great din of the wind. "We live!" roared
the replica ranks. But the beasts soared

on, buoyed by heady success, hoarding
heroes like dolls for a dollhouse. A home.

## $90K VICTORIAN, SOLD AS IS

She's trapped the rats
and thrown out lipstick,
sprinkled sugar and borax
for bugs. Sally Ann still took

the sofa, stains and all.
So that's success: steel
wool and a rickety calm.
Her bucket slops from death

to death. The apple dolls
and gas mower are gone. Same,
the orthopaedic shoes in lieu
of welcome, the seagull mobile.

She's frisked the deep freeze
for antique meats, hosed down
her granddad's hospice bed,
her hair a Celtic knot of grease.

Outside, chives take the cladding
like ivy. The once-trim garden is
raspberry bracken, dead peonies
and poppy seed heads.

Nights she slumps on the stone
front stoop, shivering lank
in granddad's sweater.
Sweet rot snacks on eaves.

BLUE-HEADS

I *had* to go and shear those craters in
my hair, locked in my bucolic boarding-
school dorm room with sewing scissors
and an androgynous ache. I was fifteen.

The local "walk-ins welcome" didn't know
what to make of my head like the moon,
so they buzzed the whole thing except for
a fringe that looked like Donald Duck's tail.

I was failing math. You were too. One day
I looked up from all the inscrutable runes
of geometry to find your grin on my threshold,
boxes of bleach and blue Hot Topic hair dye

nearly alive in your vinyl-gloved hands. I was
up for almost anything, but then I bleached
a brown towel just as blonde as my hair, so I let
you rub the blue dye in. You were used to locks

the hue of turfgrass, or purple-aquamarine, so
we didn't check the directions much, skipped
the Vaseline on my hairline and neck, so that
both and one ear held your stain for a week.

I didn't peek until both our heads had dried.
But in that moment, our hair transcended: we
were no longer bad students at a good prep
school, but blue-heads, mermaids trapped in

a New England fishbowl. We were meant
for coral, downed ships, colossal undertow.
I wanted to stay, tread water, graduate. But
somehow, once blue-haired, we had to go.

THE TOUCAN

I should have picked
the lock and set her
loose. Two free-range

American kids tended farm,
where dozens of cats
darted round our ankles

and, unbridled, the shining
hacienda horses ran free
in the Costa Rican rain,

where even the dogs
humped one another
at will (despite the influx

of touristy onlookers)
or luxuriated in their harems
of flies. But not the toucan.

She used to flit from twig
to twig of trees I never
learned to name in school,

until the farmer thought
he'd keep her as a pet.
Her call went quiet then,

her plumage damp and matted
to the touch. But in time
she almost loved her jail;

her still-wild kin sang
her karaoke daily, and,
with their din, tried

to coax her back outside.
But once so caught
by those crude wooden

bars, no bickering plea
could make her quit
her cage. Or us ours.

## THE SURGICAL THEATRE

All merry, then, in the waiting room:
I thumb *Reader's Digest* like someone'll watch
while Mum ticks her maladies off on a pad,
but swathed in her johnny shirt, she laughs.
Sister shifts on her orthopaedic foam.

We fiddle with pamphlets: lymph nodes
and the damages we do to hearts.
Madcap Medusas, in wires and electrodes,
roll past. The scritch of gauze on hurt.

Nurses tut at our slapstick smiles;
our timing's all off. But sister yells, "Flirt
for extra morphine!"
 And the hall's a grocery aisle
stocked with symptoms. Past PT, the nursery,
our Mum rolls on—the jester on her gurney.

NIGHT LUNCH

It's past 7. Even the track lights
that strip-search us daily have
soured on us now, all dimmed
post-dinner for the antipsychotic

drool-snooze of half the ward
after suppertime meds. It's 7:15.
While they sleep you tick boxes
and leave your write-in requests

for kale and raisins on the psych-
ward meal slip, flushed from an off-
unit day pass with your boyfriend
and amped for the acting class

you'll take upon discharge. It's
7:26. *No kale*, the greyish duty
nurse grumps. You scribble it
out. The hours tick by, tick us

both off. We're stuffed, but we
hunger for the backbone of ritual,
nourished by the marrow of its
repetitive motions. *Night lunch*,

the greyish duty nurse dubs it.
Cheese and crackers and single-
serve pudding they get in pallets
from a corporate food truck. You

never eat them, a holistic dietician,
but you need the snack even more
than me. It's 7:43. In a year you'll be
dead as this rumpus room with its

busted VCR, faded *Chatelaines*.
Don't ask me how. I'll have heard it
offhand and secondhand, too, from
someone with no idea I spent tonight

with you. You lecture me again on
the pudding cups I slurp. Laughing
even as you chide me, you twirl and
samba your way past the nurses'

desk. These are burdensome
halls, rooms we'll lug with us long
after we've left like plastic tiki crap
in a suitcase. It's 8. You pancake

against the wall as the locked
door bangs open. In it squeaks:
the cart of night lunch. It ferries us
diabetes with cheese. (And apples

you don't spy just yet.) In the rumpus
room the cart's unloaded into big-
ass bowls and the still-awake patients
descend on this makeshift mess hall.

*Slurp*. Finally you spy the bowl of fruit,
approach it with care like a lover you've
warred with. But when at last you bite
into that Golden Delicious, your glow

underneath the dim-bulb fluorescents
makes me glad I was this damn delirious.

MAN TO MAN

*a found poem culled from bathroom-stall graffiti*

You can smell the great
acid-rock problem from here:
smoke and shit, yes, and first-stall
action, but algo más:
all reason stinks of heaven.

God's a stalled builder of good
roads, a worker, but he's got
this boss with a bullshit
addiction and you and me
don't got the balls for a thing.

In the first stall, Natalie smells of sex.

The walls, scratched with wit
and moron advertisements,
are still here and I've still got
one bad intention. So let me
be loved. Got 3 grams of weed,

but I'm not God. We're both man-
hoes on a brewer-drunk day.
That's why the weedy roads here
aren't paved and why we say
acid rock's a real good think.

In the first stall, Natalie stinks of sex.

But God let her stink, and Kenny
Rogers holds off for the big, black
burp of acid-rock real. I love nothing
but these here drunks, the shithouse
Picassos work so hard at heaven.

## ELEGY FOR BABY GIRL

There's a girl on the bus: could
pass as your ghost, with honey-
brown skin and star-spangled

eyes. There's a girl on the bus
that goes around and around,
stopping at stops, and O how

she resembles you, her laugh
automatic, a default. But you
had no time to set a default,

no time to find fault in any
of *us*. There's a girl on the bus
who you'll never be, around

and around, with eyes that caress
whatever they look at, stopping
at stops. People get on and some

others get off. There's a girl on
the bus who looks like your shade,
if in afterlife we match who we

would have become. *Should*
have become. There's your ghost
on the bus, but she's not quite you.

It's more like a phantom pain
I get, skipping a beat in a song
I once loved. Or falling asleep

and missing my stop, skin kissing
bus-glass, as the driver pulls out
and the bus goes around and around.

MILFORD

The grown kids war
at whim again, split
their Lincoln Log
cordwood and scowl

or putt to town on Tinker
Toy exhaust. So go. Slip
away in preemie light,
the way chipmunks flit

from house to outhouse,
skittish migrants who gnaw
the nut but leave its hull
behind. The tractor's

unrepaired brake chain,
wet moss, tires, Godzilla
rhubarb the shut-down
highway store won't sell—

let lie each heirloom
and fossil bone. Past
uncles' cold-water shacks
that still lean on crossbeams,

past Share the Road
and No Trespassing
for the blueberry patch
pollinated by prayer,

walk till copse and thicket
forget and you're too far out
for bullfrogs to care. Bury
your own body in dogwood

and birch. But know when
to turn back. The grown kids
will growl you back in,
as cattails crick

from the weight of rain
and chokeweed. As men
slough the bitterness
off, a dead skin.

## BLIGHT

We freeze all those we might still
save, with flaws like blackheads
or bluish-green bruises or flecks

of cancerous skin. We can still taste
*them*, if with paring-knives-turned-
razors we dig in and eighty-six the blight

from the whole. Tomatoes. Two big
steel bowls and a black trash bag,
like picking teams for life, or gym.

The marred but not ruined go in
one bowl: dodgeball players with
bad asthma, or brides who've had

premarital sex. The other bowl is
for *les belles tomates*, tantalizingly
orange-red and squashy like stomachs—

the vine-grown, organic prima donnas.
And the black trash bag is for those
without hope. Rot, or scabs of blight

all noxious to surrounding fruit.
I came to the farm with marks
like these, my soul a putrid nugget

of gunk like the dreck that comes
when you plunge out the sink. I gather
eggs and feed the goats each day

with this gunk-nugget in mind, apologize
for each imagined wrong. I'm told
to leave the blight-marked fruit all

curbside in their plastic shroud, away
from where disease could kiss
September air and gas them all. I drag

the trash bag out to the road, but slip
and dump it in the muck of compost,
tossing bad tomatoes everywhere.

Now it's in the asparagus plants,
the trees—the whole damn farm's been
compromised. We have no choice

but to prune each leaf or sweet potato
root that holds and turf the rest. I
have to eat around the blight and live

around my black-kerneled soul. I
dream I'm a tomato we freeze and keep.
I'll cut around the blight till I feel whole.

# BIOLOGY MAJOR FIELD NOTES, 1974

    Fig. A.

*Arlo Guthrie loud as a gun, and your boy toy carts you down to the beach to watch cormorants at the salt-bleached bones of wharves.*

A slaked seventeen.
The B girls' team
you knew from school
bump and volley their ball
on Punnett squares
of bright picnic towels.

    Fig. B.

*Dry leaves; leukocytes; the orange terror of fall.*

You were in a good self
this year—went stag
to prom, a stilted rose
in your Anne Shirley hair.

But now: a soul kiss,
a pockmarked Plymouth,
and the promise you won't
grow the same as your mum.

       Fig. C.

*Her skin meat-raw from rinsing dishes in Javex, an orange cup of Tang in one crabbed, red hand.*

You are switchgrass
and barnacled shore,
skunky beer and snap
decisions, despite the dregs
of come-from-away that clot
in your knotted red mane.

       Fig. D.

*A cute boy in a Naugahyde seat cranks folk songs and points to the tide line receding back and back, the flotsam and foam, and Arlo Guthrie sings that you can get whatever you want…*

A free ride out of town. A good
volleyball serve. His nerves
all keening your name, like gulls.

## WEDDING, LATE SUMMER

It's so hot out the sumac's
flushed! They're bringing
a ham for the hall reception.
Down to chapel, your aunts

squish their skirts into pews,
pray there'll be too much
potato salad left at the end.
Mayonnaise and mercy.

Your girl cousins sneak out
for cigs in Mary Janes
that stamp like hooves,
while we fix the buttons

on this borrowed dress,
mother-of-pearl lined up
like a backbone.
(Mum sewed them on,

at first, for my sister,
but her fiancé showed up
soused and spelled his name
in breakfast on the lawn.)

Your granddad ambled with *me*
to the altar like a black bear
starved of fish. I loved
his carved pipe of bastard

tobacco, his scribble
of beard, the way my Victrola
knew as much about music
as I knew of him. But whenever

we touched he was like
a spooked fox run away
from a coyote too hurt
to catch him. When we kissed

he was newsprint pulping in rain.
But don't worry, love. You'll do it
different. Soon you'll drag your train
through mulch and the roadside

gossip of crickets' September.
Embarrass the groom, if need be,
to love him, the way your cousins
outside smoke their cigs.

They don't give a damn
for your musty union—only
for sex and sacred tobacco
burned as its fuel, like coal.

## FAIRY TALE IN THE SUPERMARKET

Now, all out of biodegradable
bags, our brave heroine (rarely seen
by day) hunches her way through

that bloated bodega, the Store.
The cart corrals clang in indecent
chaos. And what wicked spell

makes sliding doors open, close?
The Store flyer touts a sale on
turnips. But look over there, in

the culled citrus grove—*look*—
the girl slinks lithely through
the limes, in her Edwardian hairdo

and ersatz moccasins. Could *she* kill
the curse? Could they do crosswords
together, coo unknown blues to each

other by moonlight? No. The girl
turns as the quick enchantment breaks.
Our heroine hefts her cart with the bum

wheel brighter and brighter through
the Store. (Fluorescent lights make her
blink like a mole.) The meat all gleams

like battalion bits beneath its dense
zodiac of deli signs, and the tank
of lobsters who wear rubber bands

as funeral corsages are spookily still.
They've given up. But wait: over there,
by the "natural" wieners—*wait!*—the girl

again. She cradles a chunk of baloney
like a baby, her hair cropped close,
white house paint on her pants. The girl!

At last, the girl! Our heroine feels
the curse almost quit. But the girl
plunks the half-meat down in her

cart, then cuffs the ass of the boy
beside her, as though they are not in
the Store, not surrounded by clerks

and mastabas of Store-brand saltines.
Our heroine wrenches her rickety
cart away from the couple caressing

in Deli. She picks up cumin, a pillow
of oats, a free Dixie cup of marbled
cheese from a sphinx-like woman

who asks what she needs. It's like half
a riddle in Swedish or Dutch. At last,
she finds the compost bags, but they

are all too short, too wide, or too long.
And none are right for landfill conditions.
The curse makes everything feel wrong.

# MOON, MOON, EARTH

1.

I thought I'd take a walk and
have a boo at the moon, allegedly
closer than it appears tonight

in the mirror of my decrepit
corneas. The Earth's corneas.
But man, what a—*bleep!*—

disappointment! The bug-eyed
disc is only bits bigger than last
month's full enchilada (like a girl

who bloats on her menstrual cycle,
or a weightlifter whose 'roids
give him milligrams more mass).

2.

Just last week I watched you get
elected—an astonishing tide as
the moon stripped off its G-string

of cloud. The exit polls say it was
hunger for change. I don't—*bleep!*—
know. They loot and riot in each major

metro, like Trojan women setting
their own ships ablaze. Our rhythm's
all off, because even the go-tos

we know can shift (a boy who bloats
on his menstrual cycle, or an ancient
who mapped out an alternate sky).

3.

I saw a livestream of Earth from space,
so far-off that all the borders dissolved
into one big, bluish Kumbaya glob.

But did the live comments feed care?
"Hi, I'm God." "—*Bleep!*—" Swastika.
Pot leaf. "Are we over Sweden yet?"

"Sweden sux!" We shout to not think
of the censors shredding the—*bleep!*—
press in each gorgeous blue country.

I'd vote for the whole hot-hearted Earth,
but I am small (like a weightlifter whose
'roids give her milligrams more mass).

## HOARDERS: VALLEY OF THE KINGS

Pharaoh, *I know*, but you can't take it
with you. I get you're a God here in Egypt,

that it took the slaves decades to shape
your immaculate tomb. But I hear you want

it brim-full of mummified cats, their necks
all cracked so they can chase you forever?

And in matching gold sarcophagi? *Really?*
Fine. But what about the gold chair—no,

the other one, with the garish lapis
lazuli armrests—surely you can sit

somewhere else ever after? After all,
you don't want to be a scribble of paint

by a rough hieroglyph of your name. You
want that alterna-afterlife, fame, like Ramses

with his expansive franchise of sequels,
or Akhenaten and his awkward shakeup

of God. You strain for celebrity, Pharaoh,
not hoarding gold in your crotchety crypt

as you wait for a flood-plain drought to pass.
And another. Soon the death you live for

will come: no more delusions invading your brain,
your brain tugged out through your nostrils,

your nostrils stopped up by peppercorns,
peppercorns pickling your innards in jars—

your *innards*, Pharaoh! But yet you order
more deities daubed on the walls, more

proto-selfies with Anubis or Bast, more
gold urns of interred house pets for far-off

grave robbers to nab?
      Fine. We'll book you.
But don't gloat about wealth. No more slaves,

and stick to only one wife. "Pharaoh" is dicey—
call yourself "Chief," or, if you must, "The King."

And when the cameras come, recall that left's
your best side, and you're just in the pilot.

They'll try not to shoot at the Egyptian sun.

## ANALYTICS

Maybe the pigeons, manic
overeaters, peck too much
at their Pollock of used gum.

Maybe we try too hard to break
ancient gossip into gears and ions
(something *tangible*) the way

off-white LED backlights dissect
the progress of the coming train.
If we need to know which train

arrives, it's because the half-
light spurs us to separate fable
from witnessed fact. We need

data to file under Arguments
Against, charts to map a history
thick with theory: midges born

from rotten meat, gunpowder
in the elixir of life. We need
to be certain of people, of poems,

of sundry uncertain things. But
the pigeons peck. The half-light
beckons. That train is a silver question.

NURSE OUCH

is in the groggy kitchen grinding
a.m. pills to powder. She still hums
the lullabies from last night, same
as you sang her in 1965—nursing
her fever better, kissing the ouch
away. They're your lullabies, now.

She checks your adult diaper now,
tucks you in each night. The grind.
But morning trickles in. Nurse Ouch
brings you oatmeal, daybreak's hum.
You tell her she shoulda been a nurse
and she laughs. (She tried, the same

way she *always* tries—the same
hope, same let-down.) Yours for now,
she spoon-feeds you gruel to nurse
you back to—what? She grinds and grinds
her teeth at night as the radio hums.
You spit out porridge, bellow, "OUCH!"

and she hunts around for any maybe ouch-
inflicting thing. But it's always the same:
there's nothing. *Ouch* is what you hum
to her in place of conversation, since now
your words are like what a meat grinder
leaves. And constantly you call out, "Nurse!"

You feel like a baby she's slowly nursing
who won't latch on, brings a world of ouch.
When she used to fall down on the ground,
you'd kiss her bruise. It'll never be the same
again, your octogenarian skin purple now,
*more* bruised. Still Nurse Ouch is humming

carols. Even changing you, she hums!
She is medic, cook, your daughter, nurse,
and many things besides. But quiet, now.
Before you drift asleep you shriek out, "Ouch!"
again. She can tell it doesn't sound the same.
You dream that you have gone to ground

and she hums your dirge. You feel an ouch
as you nurse her at each breast, the same
she feels as now she nurses you to the ground.

HOUSE, KEPT

The oil tank sputters out of time
with the radio rumbling out its soft
jazz provocations, out of sync
with the slo-mo drip in the roof
(which soaks ceiling tiles and
makes them fragile as sandcastles).
The house has been stripped
and deloused like an inmate, but
still the mice leave their turds in
the cookware. It's been gutted
and prepped for sale, and again,
but who wants to buy a shell,
a mean ghost? Even full of couches
from 1985, it's empty. The lone
kid who stayed turns the radio
up full blast, smells old Avon
tubes she finds, watches the spot
on the kitchen ceiling as it spreads.

RECEIVING

And now you heave
your pallets of the dead,
their shucked-off husks

all gifted to Science
to help the hungover
who would be doctors:

a fatty liver's calcified
ridges, like Rockies
the size of a fishbowl

fort; the neat sortilege
of brittle old-man bones.
In class, they'll name

and groom the cadavers
like house cats, but you
do rounds of your own,

like the night you said
you'd split for the bar
"just after this album,"

but got blazed, forgot
that eight-tracks loop back
around for hours. Again

you traipse the bulk
of bodies in silence
past the med school's

bleached-lancet labs,
shipper/receiver for
a ghastly cargo. Again

you label the unlucky
rodents, their natural
labcoats white as spittle,

and again…At last you
twitch awake in a hospital
bed. An IV juices you

up with Lasix, your
arms julienned where
the nurse jabbed it in.

They bring morphine
so you float in a mint-
green haze, and med

students from back then
scrub in as your surgeons.
Bright lights, your pink

offal-guts on a screen,
and once again you
heave your pallets

of the dead at 4 a.m.
past doors like decisions.
Quiet, sterilized clean.

SPRING CATALOGUE

Bracken and hulled nuts in half-up houses.
Sweet-whiffed rot. Names carved in doors.
A porch of tar paper, melted to one mound.
Shoved-off shovels. Nails rusted rare.

A jerry can. A lawn-chair frame.
A black barbeque, black bark, and weeds.
Half-heard birds on a lake slow with scum.
The great black cabin. The lake spread wide.

A dirty bulb that hums, dim, from wire.
Where beams break through, a shade of gnats.
The synth of satellites and far-off foghorns.
A dozen spring peepers' lovesick throats.

*Popular Mechanics*. A teacup of ticks.
Unmarked, corrosive cans. A courage.
Six beds: worms, wrapped up in quilts.
Big 8 grape pop, a '94 vintage.

Low roof—makes you long for less height.
Sears & Roebuck TP. A diner table.
A stray queen of diamonds weather-beat to wood.
The worse-off wood stove and chipped blue kettle.

A book of matches too wet for fire.
A cardboard box from Nan's last move.
Twigs, and a hail-hammered sense of *here*.
Rust like bronze armour in light you could love;

beams that break on shining flies.
Pulp magazines' mail-in miracle ads.
The spring peepers' hope: their mating call.
A ready kettle. Six beds, all made.

The sweet of clover in with scum.
A white sink under a dusty layer.
A foundered rowboat full of rain.
The Book of Common Prayer.

## THE DEAD OF WINTER

"Whack set-up, yo." A live one spits
in half-thawed dirt by a park bench dupe
that reads "Sir John A. Macdonald,"

whose icicle crown melts down his face
like tears. *Around here,* the live ones joke,
*you only name winners once the snow*

*clears away.* O diesel-streaked snow.
O shawarma-shacks-cum-laundromats
that powder the folds of this city (town?)

like talcum, you can't fry enough taters
to make the live ones forget us.
We are as old as the breath on their necks

as they creak up the stairs with no one
behind them. We've been here since
before the shirtless old man a block up

the street first stripped to watch *Maury,*
his then-greying chest hair lit
cathode-ray blue. O shirtless old man,

this city (?) is like you: a giant disrobed
and forced to watch the same docudrama
for 200 years. We were here when

these ice-slick one-horse streets held
actual horses with bridles and bits,
not sidewalks so slim that fat couples

pass single file like funeral processions.
In this place, whosoever dies becomes us,
their names shorn from them like a buzz cut

shears hair. We've been here since the first
(baby? man?) quit breath, since this place
was christened (!) and then colonized

like a gut. We grew pre-war, then more post-
every-war. O green army men on the cenotaph
statue, you are all post-war. All part of us now.

Like this hard brute of a snowstorm coming.
Tomorrow, a live one in a dead goose
parka will deftly shovel the dog-pissless

white out the end of her potholed driveway,
then swear as the snowplow fills it back in
again. *Around here, you only name winners*

*once the snow clears away*. And we are
that snowplow, blinking on-off orange.
O, we are the impossible snow.

NOTES AND ACKNOWLEDGMENTS

Thanks to the following for permission to reprint:

"Best Possible Life Questions" (in a slightly different form), "13," and "Blue-heads" have all previously appeared in *Plenitude* (plenitudemagazine.ca).

"First Death in Nova Scotia, 1997" and "$90K Victorian, Sold As Is" have appeared in *Room* magazine.

"Steeltown Songs," "Step—," and "Milford" have all previously appeared in *The Puritan* (puritan-magazine.com); "Steeltown Songs" has also been anthologized in *The Best Canadian Poetry in English 2015* and *The Best of the Best Canadian Poetry in English*.

"Home Bus" has previously appeared in *Prairie Fire*.

"Man to Man" has previously appeared in *The Found Poetry Review* (www.foundpoetryreview.com/volume-three/man-to-man-sadie-mccarney).

"Analytics" has previously appeared in *Grain*.

"The Dead of Winter" has previously appeared in *The Malahat Review*.

"The Battle Re-enactors' Edda" and "Wedding, Late Summer" have previously appeared in *The Antigonish Review*; "Hoarders: Valley of the Kings" is forthcoming from the same publication.

"Last Summer at Melmerby Beach" is forthcoming in *The City Series #8: Charlottetown* chapbook from Frog Hollow Press.

"Unscattered" has appeared in *The Walrus*.

Sadie McCarney's poetry has appeared in *Plenitude, Grain, Prairie Fire, The Malahat Review, The Puritan, Room,* and *The Best Canadian Poetry in English,* among other places. This is her first book.

ᐅᓄᑲ

## OSKANA POETRY & POETICS
### BOOK SERIES

Publishing new and established authors, Oskana Poetry & Poetics offers both contemporary poetry at its best and probing discussions of poetry's cultural role.

Jan Zwicky—*Series Editor*
Randy Lundy—*Acquisitions Editor*

*Advisory Board*

Roo Borson
Robert Bringhurst
Laurie D. Graham
Louise Bernice Halfe

Tim Lilburn
Daniel David Moses
Duane Niatum
Gary Snyder

*For more information about publishing in the series, please see:*
www.uofrpress.ca/poetry

PREVIOUS BOOKS IN THE SERIES:

*Measures of Astonishment: Poets on Poetry,*
presented by the League of Canadian Poets (2016)

*The Long Walk,* by Jan Zwicky (2016)

*Cloud Physics,* by Karen Enns (2017)

*the book of ayâs,* by Neal McLeod (2017)

*The House of Charlemagne,* by Tim Lilburn (2018)

*Blackbird Song,* by Randy Lundy (2018)

*Forty-One Pages: On Poetry, Language and Wilderness,*
by John Steffler (2019)

CPSIA information can be obtained
at www.ICGtesting.com
Printed in the USA
BVHW030034211119
564400BV00001B/8/P